LEYTON GREEN

Michael Clements

PublishAmerica
Baltimore

Cover design from a batik ensemble THE CAVE OF THE FATES by the author, as are the b/w illustrations in the text

PublishAmerica has allowed this work to remain exactly as the author intended, verbatim, without editorial input.

Softcover 9781462658800
PUBLISHED BY PUBLISHAMERICA, LLLP
www.publishamerica.com
Baltimore

Printed in the United States of America

This book is dedicated to my favourite daughter,
Grabielle

Best Wishrs
for 2014,
and for a Labour
victory in 2015 !

Michael leans

Table of Contents

The Revised Infernal Almagest

Beneath the earth the battered Titans snore
outwitting the aeons and the passing
of crude time and not all the dull tapping
of Vulcan's mining elves can shake their door.
Sometimes men will turn a corner before
looking where they are, or where they're falling,
and hear the crack-head Sirens calling,
and find THAT PLACE where the worst demons gnaw.

Never leave base without the *Almagest*,
for it may guide all to safety, but know
that nothing else can, as this A to Z
of Hell was put together by the best
torn hands in the business and many bled
to revise it. (So buy, but don't borrow.)

Crystal Moth

The megrim, shankles and spotty navel-ring

are bad to catch when you are slumbering:

but even in the forest you may be stung

by the crystal moth where mistletoe has hung

and so pass out in a deep and deadly swoon

not reawakening until another noon.

Once she had lovely spangled wings.

and wove a path where the skylark sings,

but her scabrous lover stole all her rings,

and danced off down the highway to a silent tune,

leaving her to blow-jobs, blow-outs and blokey blows.

And so, capering where the mistletoe grows,

appeared her saviour, a highly respected local pimp,

termed by all the "Prince of Turnips"

when, all in white, he served boiled beef and carrots

on cut-price Ukrainian Black Sea cruising ships.

Numbered among the chuck-chuck chucked-up, chucked-
out fools,

those mutual bum-boil bursting crackers of verbal pustules,

he taught her how to draw cakes to allay hunger,

how to wrestle in mud for florins with Logrolling Lola,

and how to smell out skips with buried treasure:

then, at last old and ugly, she couldn't pleasure

even a half-blind senile evangelist in a sorely tempted plight.
Yet true to say, Crystal Moth and her Prince of Pods
settled down in unmarried bliss, and the whimsical gods
were pleased to compound their autumnal delight
by turning them into giant Carboniferous dragonflies
hovering in an eternal mating dance in the endless night.

The Hero Has Grown Wings

I have to dodge the venomous glances
of Gorgo and her sisters if I am to save
the maiden on the rock, and kill the dragon.
From the sea it comes, the revenge of Poseidon,
and all the Fates would conspire
to see this hero prince perish in its fire
for the sake of a truly uninspiring desire.
In my right hand I hold the lightning,
and in my left the goatskin bag of the winds.
Riding upon the black clouds of storm
But if it devours a girl dragged each dawn from her bed
think what savings fair Joppa would make
in refuse collection, if we could train it to take
the left-overs from the meat market instead.

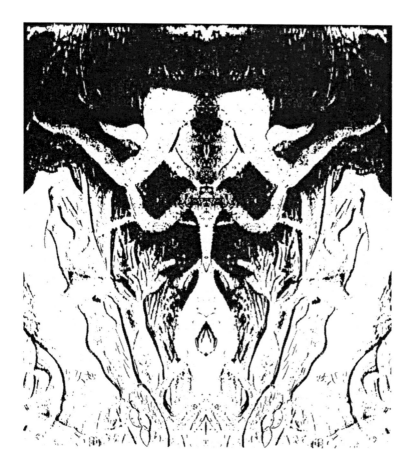

Moonlight Casts Strange Shadows

Behind my garden wall
half invisible waits the cat
with the gladness
of the spring hunt:
the full moon
speaks of hunters
and cracking twigs
and we long for tigers
to tear the silence
with the cough
of dedicated interest
that comes from a lean belly.
But this is not the Seoni Hills
and the silver lady
must stay disappointed.
We all love to catch a rat
and splinter bone
with our hungry teeth,
spit out blood
and soiled hair,
and gulp down the rest,
but cannot manage
a grown sambhur buck....

But this is a famous treacle pudding night
when even cats may have
an out of the body experience
and bound through a Rousseau landscape.
I hear the syrinx whistle
when the dark dreamer in the shadows
calls forth sensual dreams
and sweaty clutchings
and rhythmic bush shaking:
the moon is a magic lady
and can create kittens
out of the night air.

Palm Wine Woman Juggles the Moon

On the cliff edge
she looks down
on our star-lit huts
and the breeze
twitches the long ears
she cut off a slain boar.
Like a ghost she'll slip
under your roof.
When her left hand smears
fresh menstrual blood
on your spears
while you kip,
then your family
will all go hungry
for a month.

You must leave
food on a leaf
and palm wine
for her too,
if you are wise.
Then at moonrise
she will dance above

the village of men
and grant a blessing.

Some say she's the last
of the people who lived
here before; others
that she's a spirit
thrown out of heaven,
or escaped from hell.
Some don't care
but all know
that one day she'll go,
or just not be there,
leaving us to sleep
without her nightmare.

Leave the Forest

Leave the forest
and the laughing stream,
leave the sounds
of children at play
under the watchful eyes
of big sisters in disguise.
Cross the endless plain
where leopards hunt
and always light a good fire
before the stars come out.
Then one day as it goes,
you will see the spear spire
and the three rocks
like a lion with two cubs
and know that the great
river is very close.
Will you stop here and think:
"Now shall I return home
and boast that these hands
have stroked the three beasts
of red stone?"

You could bring back
a little red flake
and be counted a man
by your entire clan.

Or will you go on,
and drink from the river?
Will you defy the dragons
who live in it, hide in it,
waiting not in vain
for the brave who cross the plain.
For, remember,
once you have drunk
that magic water,
you'll see things anew,
and may never want
to return to unknowing
happiness again.

Solon the Wise

Solon built saloons
and was called the Wise when he
provided spitoons.

Dagenham Smiles

The googly poodle loved by Brenda's mum
has snatched her blue netball knickers and vest
from the saggy line and run away west,
chased by Brenda needing to cover her bum
from the lecherous stare of Dagenham.
O magpies glaring down from your high nest
please intercept the nightly yelping pest
and make of this schoolgirl a lifelong chum!
Like stukas they swoop and knock him down
then grab the dry but no longer clean clothes
and return to their perch with crafty looks.
Squirrels in the tree, stop playing the clown,
as a reward she'll nut on nut dispose:
"Or are all you creatures a bunch of crooks?"

Churchill

His name means Boots in Turkish:
he had a long tongue and a worn soul,
and was something of a heel,
as he tramped around South Africa,
cleverly not seeing the British death camps full
of starving women and children;
though he later thought it rich
to drive a ditch
across Ireland and stamp the Irish down,
behind another barbed wire fence.
He jumped all over the Welsh miners,
and called Gandhi a naked beggar
for walking in bare feet along an East End street
draped in a cottton sheet.
Then he tripped himself up by confusing a thousand years
for the British Empire with a thousand days;
he painted silly watercolours and wrote unreadable tracts
about his ramshackle empire, and at Yalta, laughing fit to tears
Uncle Joe and FDR tied his laces together
and watched him fall into the dustbin of history.
When the returning warriors of the Eighth Army
voted him out of power, his ruddy relatives screamed treason!

all waiting for the other boot to fall,
red English faces turning blue,
but Mountbatten's eventual coup
never came off, and we, the people, at least for a time, won.

A Quick-Fried Rigmarole

Sinister men are lowering their trousers
as light fades from the Hornchurch skies.
their soft white hands seeking the comforts
of a rigid baseball bat, watery eyes
becoming hard and drug-debased.
Dirty shirts cling all up-rolly
to sweaty paunches and unchanged boxer shorts:
they want to join the unelected magistrates
prowling the night on the backs of whores,
hurling bricks through citizens' windows
and kicking in tower block doors.
Such men with moustaches and shaven pates
bring flatulence where the privet hedge grows;
such men gorge on tripe when the strawberry is ripe,
and pour custard on fried Mars bars, and swipe
little squares of tomato sauce from police canteens
to suck while they peruse pornographic magazines;
such men would sell their vote for half a crown,
watch, unmoving, old ladies, little kids and kittens drown;
such men have been stuck in middle-age since their teens.

Every night they seek on their mobiles the rich enchanter
with the quizmaster hair-do to beg him for luck in life,

but he will only conjure for some other sponger in skirts
with authentic prison tattoos, or some backstreet lounger
who has honed his skills as a TV scrounger,
and those losers who once dreamed of leading Blackshirts
must, with shoulders lowered, face an angry wife.

The Huntress

Artemis, fair Leto's daughter hunted
for rats with a big blow-pipe, an easy prey,
and with a dreadful yell, most every day
she hurled them puffed and bloody away,
into the yard of our neighbourhood school.

Such behaviour made her sporty brother look a fool!
Taking her aside with a patronising smile,
Captain Apollo in his cricket whites said: "Sister dear, while
I admire your fearful accuracy,
and your frightening skill in slaying, see,
I believe that massacring the world's creatures
is one of life's more unseemly features,
best left to huntsmen with horrid dogs,
-girls should do needlework and make nice togs,
flirt with sailors, and act sweet and charming,
not hunt down rodents and be alarming!"

Muddy and dishevelled, the divine child
glowered up at him, but her tone was meek:
"If I don't do the buggers in, no-one will.
Save your strictures for the middle-classes,
and all that give the rats a chance pig-swill,

for in a dump like this where life is war,

hunting rats is the highpoint of my week,

though I'd prefer to inter those braying asses

who promise me the love of Jesus at the door.

Pan's People

Before us were the Titans,
and before the Titans in their pride,
there lived Pan's People,
and they created the whole lot.
They also moved aside,
with much puffing and panting,
anything that seemed in their way,
dumping it into the non-place,
non-time, non-somethingness with a damp smell,
making anti-time and anti-space,
filled up from uncle's cellar to auntie's attic,
full of antiphonic creaking: a sort of Hell
called Chaos, or Rub al-Khali, like that dried up pond
beyond the Black Stump where Essex
finds itself mirrored, shadowy and melodramatic.
Thus they made a lasting testimony
to the quirkiness of it all,
a quirkiness which is totally human
because it's so imperfect,
because humans thought of it first,
and gave it a reason to thirst.

Great Pan Himself was given the two charms:
that of doing and that of undoing,
from his mother, the Universe,
and taught them to his son,
Merlin, who sat on his daddy's knee,
his eyes bright and shining.
I cannot reveal the charms,
but only say they are pure simplicity
to use but carry a great curse
for inept meddlers, which I'm sure you know.
They also have to be sung,
not spoken, and accompanied
by that same dance performed
by the First Ancestors.

"Wisdom fruit is not for sale,"
The Lord of the Forest told his son,
and "Find your soul,
or spend forever
dead.
Watch the cats
because they
know.

Everything began
in the middle
and will end
at the beginning.

The ancestors
smelted rocks
and sang mountains
into existence.

Sand painting
is the key
to knowledge,
and time can be blown
away with the coloured
grains—leaving the self.

Everything is a mandala
centred on ourselves:
everything is part of a grand dance,
and when the drums lower their voices,
the panpipes raise the tempo.
Beloved is the goddess with black hair
who uses the *mudras* to draw us in,
and blessed is the watcher at the door

who can enter the eternal dream,
and join her on the threshing floor.

All that is human ends up on the burning grounds,
all that is immortal has no bounds"

The Great God Pan smiled paternally,
and bounced little Merlin on his knee:
"Heaven and Earth are without limit.
When you hear the gongs clashing
and see the red pillar-boxes turning
like prayer-wheels, remember that those
who created the universe by poetry, not prose,
discovered the Charm of Doing
and are our ancestors, and our very own kin."

He went on: " There was Bald Pot Leaf,
Sore Slip Slope, and Bad Ugh! Bing
among the men, and among the women,
Cool Jug Glug, Green Snake Skin,
and Glue High Snoot. They were all tired
of the gloomy forest full of dangers
and resolved to leave, like homeless strangers,
hiking to the sea-shore, naming the world
as they went." The little one's eyes grew big.

Pan went on: "They danced and sang,
nailing everything into their minds, neatly furled,
with the power of human thought, bang!
This power of dance, as I have taught you,
my little big-eyed toddler,
is the greatest force in the cosmos."

At this point Merlin gripped his daddy's nose
and squeezed. Merlin said: "Don't do that!"
and brushed aside the little fist.
Instantly, the child put it back
and resumed his squeezing. For some time
father and son developed a sort of seated dance,
hand and fist moving almost too fast to see,
until, despairing of freedom,
Pan resumed his talk with a drone
like an adenoidal Persian shah
upon his golden peacock throne:
"Now, Bad Ugh! Bing had a plan
to put his hot, hairy palms all over lovely
Cool Jug Glug, the dirty old man!
But when he jumped out at her unexpectedly
from behind a bush, flashing without restraint,
the blushing maiden fled back to camp
and summoned the others to witness her complaint:

"He's always trying to pinch my bum!
And makes unseemly kissing sounds
when I walk past with a female chum-
his impropriety knows no bounds!"
And the fair flower of the dusty savannah
invited all to examine the bruises on her rear-
which, tut-tutting, they did, no fear!
And such intent mind force from a group hug
altered the brave blue world and Cool Jug Glug,
who became the first Femme Fatale, I deem,
or in Schiller's bright, romantic scheme:
das ewig Weibliche, no better wedding planner!
Next day Bald Pot Leaf too became an archetype:
blue smoke led him to a lightning blasted tree
still smouldering with red embers.
These he collected and created for a laugh
a portable flame provider,
becoming thus the inventive Magician.
Sore Slip Slope poked the camp fire
with his fruit-dislodging staff
when they all lay down to kip,
and forgot to pull it out again.
Next morning the blackened tip
was hard and sharp -as a hidden leopard found
dropping from a tree to pin

Sore Slip Slope to the ground.
The big cat died disbelieving
and the man lived to be the Hero in its skin.
In the coming days, as the people
named all the trees and brooks, the rocks,
the plants and forest flowers, and fishes in the pool,
some became glorious templates
for the human spirit, and all earned a place
as the Ancestors who created our Universe,
and even Bad Ugh! Bing found his niche
as the universal butt of jokes, or Fool.

Great events cast their shadows both forward
and back, and all this naming (and shaming)
consumed all origins with a purpose made inherent
and which now races ever onward to completion, still unspent.

The Universe yawned, woke up, put on Her dress
of black and silver, adjusted Her shining crown
of nebulae and said: "*AUM!* What a mess!"
For our ancestors, being human,
had left the cosmic equivalent of mud pies,
and grubby fingerprints across the glorious skies.
With the sacred syllable awoke the Great Jinn,
those star-born beings formed of pure energies

who hate disorder and who all then turned and glared
at Her with disapproving eyes, pointing at the spilled dustbin.
The Universe decided to make Herself scarce
for an aeon or two, and was straightway born the daughter
of Cool Glug Jug and Sore Slip Slope,
and because she was a new sort of baby,
less hairy and with a high forehead,
her mother gave her a secret name: Ma,
though she called her in public: Eve Star Song.
And when the tribe sang brown girl in the ring
over her, she giggled and tried to sing along.
so that one and all laughed and called her the cutest little thing!
The Great God Pan paused and sighed
as Merlin released his nose: " Ma was my mother,
your paternal grandmother, who holds everlastingly
in henna-painted hands, all we are or can ever be."
Merlin belched and giggled,
Pan tickled him until he wriggled,
and both laughed and laughed exceedingly.

Floreat E10er

The school doctor introduced me to it
at an early age, noticing the bulge
in my shorts—all that learning might divulge
of delight she matronly gave me. Wit
and innocence of curiosity split
my personality.
Teachers regard
such precocity as evidence (hard
to dispute) of a dirty mind, a pit
to trap the unwary. When the woodwork
master surprised me with a manic glare
in sawdust reddened eyes, I escaped with a tear
in my undershirt. Thus I learned to lurk
in the academic shadows, keeping
my parts private and libido sleeping.

Xmas Tanka

The fierce wind brings sleet from the north
scattering the slates from my roof;
night will hide safe roads, stain the snow
with the blood of many Santas.

Meat Pie Land

While his staff watched aghast,
the Emperor Claudius ate a huge pork pie
with an egg cooked in the middle.
" I say, is this a local d-d-dish?" stuttered
the old boy in his purple cloak,
"I find it rather t-t-tasty."
A legate shuffled his feet and muttered:

"Don't offer him the custard cremes
as they'd make a Harpy croak,
and that dreadful toad-in-the-hole
would give Medusa nasty dreams."
The imperial cook fell on a tribune's sword
when Claudius called for spotted dick,
but, unperturbed, the stuttering Caesar
hired local dinner ladies
and took them back to Rome
to prepare banquets for celebrities;
though Herod of Judaea took amiss
the tripe and onions seethed in milk,
declaring independence as soon as he got home.
Some aver that the flatulent emperor
was poisoned by his queasy wife,

but what really carried him off before time
were some half-cooked rissoles,
for the ladies had never mastered
the art of cooking in a hotter clime.
At least Nero's blow-outs made him highly popular
in comparison, for he replaced the Britons
with Italian chefs, all celebrity taste-teasers.

And the despondent dinner ladies,
returning home, perked up a bit
after opening fast food outlets bearing signs:
Purveyors of Delicacies to the Caesars.

No Bindle Stiff Cringers

All day we crouched over our bindles,
working away with the weaving spindles,
together united, Frank, a time-expired nuthouse cobbler,
Phil, the outed race-horse nobbler,
and Silly Mary the half-wit with a noble soul,
who served us all chicken soup in a communal bowl,
while we raced to complete
the homeless man's new interview suit
out of an NHS hospital winding-sheet.

The Ongarites burst into the shed
waving baseball bats and baling hooks
and tried to disrupt our unholy endeavour,
calling upon their Con of Man,
Sid of Becontree Heath, Master of the Never Never,
to recite a curse from his sacred tally-books,
because we wouldn't buy his shoddy,
but brave Mary dropped their leader dead
when she bent her iron sauce-pan
on his goo-matted and unwashed head,
and all the rest fled back 'cross the Roding
to their sties, resentful wives and credit card decoding.

The magically summoned Primate of Worms
snuck in like a snake through the back,
that peddler of true confessions, Snogga Heldhand,
who preached the Gospel according to Jack,
clad in the horsehair nightshirt of his band,
a Thatcherite who hated co-operative manufacturing firms.
He was seeking to baptise in blood us bindle-fardlers
with a whacking two foot monkey-wrench,
but an avalanche of oil-drums almost had him canned,
and he retreated back down the weedy track.
And all his tipsy dipshit twits in their tapestry caps
were not up to the fight with a single crabpaste
sandwich snacker, high as a kite on stolen smack,
our backdoorman, Olaf of Bergen, and they gave up the attack.

Last of all, Filthy Freddy, the fish-shop chip fryer,
came marching in with his slavering dogs from the waste,
demanding rent from us vision quest dossers,
but the suit lay completed in candid glory, and we rose up
in ire,
like true Workers of the World and murdered the tossers:
Silly Mary and her Bacchae tore those whining dogs apart,
and Phil ripped out the quivering fatso's heart.
We stuck his gaping head on a sharpened broomstick,
a sight to make any passing monarchist sick,

and marched around the ill-chosen Olympic site,
singing "ça ira, ça ira!" giving the gaffers a nasty fright!

When we got to the High Road we were only ten,
marching behind the Messianic white suit,
but then we were joined by some silly old men
who used to be the band (long ago) of the Boy's Brigade,
and they insisted that "Tipperary" instead be played,
not knowing the words of the Revolutionary Hymn.
When we entered Walthamstow, we were a few thousand,
but when we stood 'neath that hateful Pyramidion[1]
we were in our tens of thousands. We trashed
the middle-class necropolis, dragging the embalmed mummies
from their pine-wood and fake satin lined boxes,
stacking them up to burn in the Chapel of Rest Arcade,
sometimes staging them in filthy tableaux like sex dolls
and dummies,
then laughing, we lit up Walthamstow like Attila, on a
shopping day-trip,
and to the light of the luxurious flames we brought up
mobile cranes
from the new library site, and lassooed the obelisk with chains.
As it crashed to earth, the sarcophagus was propelled by
the shock
through the glass like a shell from Big Bertha, and was
about to splash

1 refer to "The Margaret Thatcher Pyramidion and Necropolis" to be published
later

down into slime-bleeding Tottenham Reservoir when a monstrous croc

rose from the black waters and swallowed whole the leader and the four

all under one lid: this was Sobek, the Devourer of Evil Hearts,

with a great crunch and gulping roar, performing his famous nip.

Then we lit up the sky while our masters fled, we the ignored, the doubted,

the troubadors of sorrow, the oppressed and nameless mass,

the enemy within who subsist beneath the greedy mad old women

and sexless, withered dukes with German titles and Norman blood,

and it was wonderful to dance on those hostile bones and kick

our enemy's servants' empty skulls around the blazing neighbourhood.

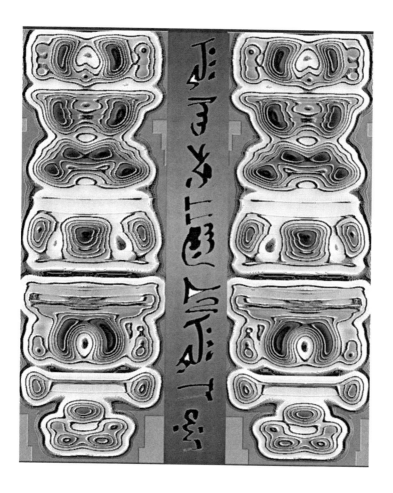

Scarlet Lords and Purple Bishops

Yes! We're back again to lay down the law
all with a hearty a-haw-haw-haw,
the chinless wonders who won't go away,
the bend-over bullies with sad little willies
who'll always get the powerless poor to pay
for the lounger scrounger with a title or two!
So we thrash the beggar
for not saying please,
feel up the charlady on her knees,
get by with our air of inherited command,
certainly not elbow-grease!

We love girls' schools run by cringing fools,
sometimes leave dead rent-boys in swimming pools,
the occasional watery grave for sods who won't behave,
but our old man's a Lord Lieutenant in the shires,
and Uncle Jack's a High Court Judge,
who thinks all working-class oiks are thieves and liars,
so we can do whatever we please.

We're going to re-conquer the world,
and are half-way to it by globalising work,
making new slaves of the Asians and blackies,

and we can play toodle-fart with the fair trade scales,

because we can rely on devoted lackies

to keep us in power and out of the jails.

So we'll steal worse than any Angevin count,

never pay taxes (an incalculable amount!)

and find each other smashing jobs by the back door,

which don't demand more than winning smiles:

because we're clever, oh so clever, a-haw-haw-haw

and the tabloids love us now, and will for ever more,

because we have oodles of class, and ancient piles.

We fill Oxford and Cambridge to keep the riff-raff out,

because our line is noble and our dads are rich,

we throw bread rolls a lot and never leave tips,

always laughing like donkeys high on smack,

we're English gents, and punch above our weight,

(provided the chauffeur holds the girl's hands behind her back.)

So God save the House of Lords, and the purple bishops too,

God save the monarchy with its strutting goat and arrogant clown,

and God save England which can never change,

till the North Sea rises and swallows it down,

and the giggling Welsh point and pray we'll all drown,

for we'll get by in Argentina, high and dry,

with Eton and Harrow rebuilt on the pampas range,

an Andean St Paul's, and Buck House moved stone by stone

to South Georgia to protect the crown.

No comeuppance for us, you can be sure!

We'll always be with you—a-haw-haw-haw!

Hot Nights

Talons dig crumbling fence posts
and cat-song complains
about the creosote crud smell,
where I have done my bit,
(if none too well)
to preserve and protect
the old wood from every lurker
in silver armour,
and the stinking fungus,
grimmer and more awful
than the rotten beard
of a senior social worker.

Last night, warned
by strident cat-song,
I intercepted Aphrodite
trying to sneak out past me:
her leatherette coat fell open
revealing no skirt and a tiny thong:
"No, you don't young lady!
Not while little Eros
has head-lice, and has wet
the bed, so neglected is he, poor pet!"

Enraged, she took a swipe at me
Thatcher-like with laden handbag,
and her son punched my knee:

"Don't you hurt my mummy!"

Falling over in my hallway,
I took in two blond,
and beautiful faces glowering
down at me, and unable to rise,
shouted up at her like one possessed:
"If you don't do what I say,
I'll tell Athena you fixed that contest
when Paris awarded you the prize!"
It was a desperate ploy,
as I didn't really know the truth,
but the effect was instant.
Her rose-petal lips made
a perfect O, from shock and fear,
and the goddess of Love,
found out as a cheat only this year,
after thirty-two hundred had passed,
meekly changed into something nice,
and washed Cupid's hair free of lice.

The Robin

Puffed up with red rage
he glares at me with hatred:
"Quick! Help! Bring the cat!"

Kali

In my right hand a sword of star-metal bones,

in my left the severed head of a world shaker:

I can clear a battlefield faster than Grace Jones,

and then dance as well as Josephine Baker.

The Two Thousand Year War

We fight the same battles
in every generation, with no hope
of seeing the golden domes of the New Babylon,
or the Long Walls of an undefeated Athens.
Once we mortals were fire and ice united
on sacred ground, and did not grovel to madmen.
So short is our memory become that our arts
have withered like a cursed fig-tree,
and our science has become the discovery
of unrelated parts, as though faith in the monstrous father
and his lying priests has replaced our eyes and ears.
When those monks, drunk with the certainties of ignorance
murdered Hypatia they condemed us all in the West
to their monkey puzzles, and when they showered
the slaves with baptismal water
they made us all accessories to the crime.
The new Dark Age waits as their creation
from the monstrous jelly of a sick constipation.
Must we give up the final victory in this war
because they have taught us to love their blind comfort more
than our freedom, and the goodies we bought
at cost from the powerless poor?
Nobody loves his god more than a Russian

billionaire, or a crafty Texan with a wall-eyed stare,
which must mean something obvious, and not nothing more.

The sleep of the middle generation
is drugged with suburban dreams and ultimate despair,
and for us few remain memories of glory. and the dare.

The Wanderer

This band of fools who walk the streets beneath
the broken teeth of London discuss me
with witless voices as a phantasy
for children, but there on Hampstead Heath
I talked to Blake who listened to the breath
of the stars and was silent. Willingly,
find me a beggar at your door, lonely
in the prison with a prophet's dreams, death
in my hands in some forgotten desert
or jungle: with Arjuna at the Field
of Kuru, or in Sultan Salah's tent
praying before Hattin—but do not flirt
with me because I am awful, and sealed
with blood, nor will I hear your argument.

Meditation Outside the Moghkadeh

The poor, tired old fiend coughs up coins
like a lucky slot machine,
while the wind from the Sahara
carries warm whispers and sand
from distant, mysterious Tatouine.
A huge silver half crown rolls into my hand
like a miniature Wheel of Ixion,
and the Devil's daughter grins
as she paints her toe-nails green.

I, who have lampooned the clowns,
jugglers, contortionists and collaborators
of Westminster, must now tell stories in the dust
of a foreign place to earn a kindly crust.
I'll not take coppers for my tales,
ha'pennies and sticky farthings,
but only shillings, silver marks,
even the five franc gilded fraud of the third
Napoleon, any coin which won't shame the scales,
even if it bear the double-headed bird
of a shameful Czar, or the seal of the Sultan.

Release now the tormented souls from the bitumen
for they only took a wrong turning in Becontree
and fell through the cracks in the pavement,
don't you see, O Master of the Dual Mystery?
I've sand beneath my finger-nails, but I haven't stirred
from my bedroom Bokhara rug. -Though I'm sure I heard
a phone ringing with news from nowhere, Tartary
(or boring Bangalore) about an offer of repentance
rewarded by the Apostate Bishop of Basildon.
Just take that bastard's soul as payment down instead!
I'll add a few black stones from the River Gandakee,
and then we can all applaud Satan for setting the innocent
free.

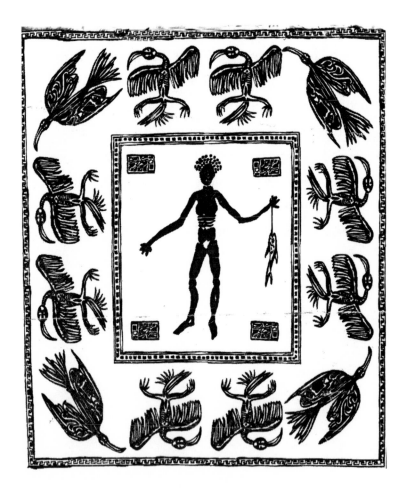

Fish Cakes for Tea

This sight I saw at midnight
in that place of rotten fruit
and old linoleum, our municipal rubbish tip,
as rats danced in their moonskin breeches
on piss-soaked bedding and black bags surged up
like a malodorous sea, beneath the shipwrecked
clouds: a witch in a trouser-suit
of red wool and her naked acolytes
in their traditional pointed black hats,
the Eves of Epping Forest,
putting a curse on their employer,
our local council, for not paying them more.
I made off home before they saw me.

I found a new dug pit, out back under the tree-roots,
and saw emerge from it a red-haired miner
all sweaty and smelly, his right leg
in a caliper of bronze, bare-chested
wearing only a leather apron and hob-nail boots.
It was, of course, the belittled Hephaestus,
building an underground workshop
for his hammering craft, his lightnings,
tipped with fulminate of mercury,
all for His Nibs, Lord Zeus, to make go pop.

He greeted me with a delighted grin,
for we belong to the same union,
and I too limp about like a ruined fiddler's bitch,
and said: " Zeus finally replied to your begging letter."

"How much did he send, and was it in euros,
or very acceptable Athenian silver staters?"
He laughed for ages. "Now, that's rich.
-It was in kind, and all provided by Poseidon, too.
But I cleared it up and put as much as poss
in your small fridge. The telchins, my green sprogs,
cleaned and salted the rest, leaving none behind,
and now half lies dry and safe in my deep cold-store,
while half is being smoked over oak chips on burning logs."

For that mean old bugger had sent this dross:
a rain of fish on my garden as a jovial jest.
But the fish-gut stench, and the circling harpies,
those bat-winged, cross-eyed hags,
who bore aloft the bulging black refuse bags
to some fearful, bone-strewn nest,
made the neighbours turn purple and rave to the police.
Even the dustbin men threatened a fine,
so I had to bribe them with ten squid apiece.

A Long Way West of the Pillars

No galley sailed these seas, only Carib
canoes and the rafts of the Arawak,
and the moon calling upon waters' slack
tides produced turtles abundantly. Rib
upon rib of a lost continent
mark Atlantis in a blue firmament
of sea starred by shark teeth and octopus
ink, insect haven of Oceanus,
coral upon Vulcan's back. All this glows
from crab claw Trinidad to Havana,
fish scaly candle-fly phosphorescent
under the eye of Scorpio: tide flows
upon brilliant strands and in this manner
grants us forgetfulness in the present.

The Great White Stone

My love ties me to the Great White Stone
with bonds of briar and ivy green,
and I am become withered and drooping
like an old man stooping
in a frost-bitten funeral scene.
For you should never wed a witch
who knows more than you do
about Baby Bio and fish bone
and where the bodies are buried.
She will have me pushing up green shoots
in the spring, using my skull
as a watering-can. That is her plan.
With a big grin she will scatter me in
the black earth, and earn a jolly year
from the fertilized soil with minimum toil.
So if you have the status of married man,
check your darling's potting shed,
for old bloodstains, axe cuts and similar wear,
lest you too enhance a wilting flower-bed.

Our Lady of Philae

After her defeat by Cuchulain,
Meadbh of the night-black hair
made herself scarce, crossed the sea to Tintagel,
boarded a Syrian trader and so
voyaged to Alexandria, seeking
new magic to revenge herself:
so chronicled the monks many years
after her assassination.

Fat Philopator, ruler of Egypt and murderer, coward
and politician liked not her look, calling her Medea
behind her back because of her witchy look,
her tattoos, the white scar from a sword-thrust
on her chin and her hairy, backslapping
bodyguard and suggested she seek help
from the ancient oracle of Isis,
on breeze-favoured Philae at the far end of his empire.
Meadbh studied the obscene mural of a naked god,
Dionysus in fact, behind the throne, and hastily agreed.
Thus, for three weeks the Nile
resounded to the anthems of Connachta
and the warriors sank jars of yellow
beer and played at quoits with arm-rings of gold,

silver and red bronze in the blistering
sun while she sipped the essence of the blue
lotus and feasted with nard in her hair,
watching the peasants till the fresh, black silt
deposited by the swollen river
in the season of *akhet* just ended,
until the boat neared the first cataract.

Until at last, Meadbh could set her slim foot
upon the dusty land, adjusting her
see-through dress of gauze, her nails painted red,
a boy bearing a parasol above
her gorgeous head and a corsage sitting
on her wrist, hiding the scar left by her
leather bowstring guard. Entering the sacred temenos
of this place so holy to great Isis,
a royal herald whispering etiquette in her ear,
she bade her grumbling escort to stay out,
to go to their quarters and snore off their
headaches, or gamble at chequers, or else
ogle the naked women painted on the walls.

The temple cats yowled to see her
and wound about her white feet, delighted
by the smell of expensive perfume

mingled with polished leather, and most of all, magic,
which she carried about her like Meadbh mist.
Egyptian cats were black and long-leggy
with small heads, like little panthers; many
wore ear-rings of bronze and onyx, alone
the Great Mother Cat of the House displayed
a collar of gold and lapis lazuli,
and she followed Meadbh closely, shadow-like
and crouched at, sometimes on, her feet, during
her interview with the High Priest, who took
his fee from the royal herald, and promised
Meadbh consultation with the oracle
in the near future, if not tomorrow.

In the days which followed, her nobles found
some old chariots in dusty storage
and prevailed upon the temple servants
with heavy tipping and ripe, beery breath
and then hired horses from the officers
of the strategos, racing each other
along the shore, shrieking like madmen, then
challenging the Greeks for prizes, piling bet
upon bet, laughing at the crashes and
pile-ups, laughing at their own broken bones,
so charming the officers and local

nobles with their heroic zest for loud
and immediate destruction that they
found themselves invited to a lion-hunt.

Meadbh joined them, wearing her best leather trews
under long shirts of silk and linen, bow
of oryx horn and yard-long arrows to
hand, her black hair bound back by a royal
fillet, under a Greek straw hat.

Once lions had freely roamed the pastures of Nubia,
hunted by mythic Pharoahs with cool names
like Amenophis and Sesostris, though
no queens went with them, but years of revolt
had left villages deserted and full
of naked bones, fields abandoned to the
hungry sands, people and game moving south
to hide beyond the second cataract.
Past the great mansions of Ozymandias
they sailed, landing at last to assemble
the chariots for the hunt. Rapaire
was the name of her charioteer, a
red-haired, boisterous youth full of capers
and funny walks when he had both flat feet
on the unyielding ground, but a shrieking

child of the wind-god with reins in his hand
and fine horses before him.

It so came
about that Meadbh and Rapaire became
separated from the rest of the hunt
after a quarrel with their hired tracker,
a tall handsome Nubian, naked but
for a crown of ostrich feathers, against
whom Rapaire took umbrage when he
pissed over the wheel of the chariot.
No doubt this was some local tracking ploy,
some way to guide the hounds to them,
should they take a wrong turn,
or some luck-bringing ceremony,
but Rapaire drew his racing dagger
with a cry of "Och, ye dirty devil!"

Before he could commit murder, their guide
made off into the sedge and elephant
grasses which flanked the river at that spot.
It was approaching mid-day and so hot
that one could cook eggs on the rocks without
need of fire: Meadbh saw a juniper tree
some little way off and they made their way

into its shade, unharnessed the matched pair
of racing greys, gave a little water
to them, drank from the goatskins and so
rested in the shade.
It seemed to the dozing queen
that the grasses bordering the Nile some
thirty feet in front of her just parted
to reveal the grinning face of
the god Dionysus staring at her with
yellow eyes, and she distinctly
heard a sly voice say in Greek:
"We have some unfinished business, Medea!"
Afterwards, she never knew if
the god had warned her of the danger, or
had intended her death out of spite.
But at once the Nile breeze faltered
in its steady up-river flow, the two
horses went crazy at the whiff of some
deadly scent, and escaped their loose halters,
making off with rolling eyes and whinnies of fear.
Rapaire fell over and began to
snore, while Meadbh's eyes suddenly flew open.
The dark face before her had become
the black-maned head of a crouching lion
which instantly sprang upon her roaring

to confuse and terrify: her weapons
were all stacked neatly against the body
of her chariot, some way out of reach,
but she seized the shaft of the parasol
grounded at her side and swung it down to
block the beast, not having time to close it,
or even aim it. In an instant a
great weight crushed the breath from her body
and she expected to feel mighty jaws
engulf her luckless hide, or huge claws dig
down to the bone—but first she felt only
a convulsive quivering above her
which made her wonder if the randy beast
were trying to screw her, and if so, his
technique seemed only a slight improvement
over that of her countrymen, but then
buckets of warm, sticky fluid gushed down
her neck, obviously blood not semen.

Later, it was apparent that the bronze
spike which tipped the parasol had buried
itself deep in the monster's brain, driving
through its gaping jaws (most fortuitous
when it came to preserving the skull as
a trophy), but for an eternity

Meadbh had to gasp for breath blinded by the
folds of material around her face
until an incompetent Rapaire
managed to lever the dead weight aside
and, white-faced, determine her injuries.

No sooner had the blood-soaked rags and spokes
of the parasol been removed, than Meadbh tried
to sit up, only to be knocked back flat
by two of the fleet dogs which had been loosed
to find them: excitedly they licked blood
from her face, tails wagging, whilst a third pissed
over the same wheel of the chariot.
They heard then distant shouts from the hunting party....

....Part of a letter from Parmenion,
herald, to Ptolemy the God, the New
Dionysus, Philadelphus etc, styled as
Philopator, but called Auletes or
the "Flute-Player" by his long-suffering
people behind his back:

My King, and my God,

Medea, Queen of the Western Islands has returned
in triumph from the hunt, single-handed
miraculous slayer of a lion,
thought almost extinct above the second
cataract, her companions slaughtering
wild pig, some few gazelles and numerous

crocodiles, turning their teeth into crude
necklaces, and their hides into belts and
boots—no doubt each of them will claim title
as Dragonslayer on his return home.
Medea stepped ashore at Philae, the cured
hide of the beast draped over her shoulder,
her long hair bound by a royal fillet
of white wool, tall, lovely, commanding, eyes
flashing, and the people ran to throw at
her feet the flowers of the blue lotus,
crying: *"Amenti-Wa'aset! Sat-Ra,
Amenti-Wa'aset!"* in the old
language hailing her as the great Isis
of the West, daughter of Ra.
Many of the sons of the local nobility
and royal officers have asked me to
propose marriage on their behalf and I
have finally persuaded the high priest
to bring forward her interview with the
goddess to avoid worse entanglements,
bearing the volatile situation here in mind.

When the letter was received
by Philopator, he groaned and wept, and
took another pull on his wineskin, then

arranged passage for the Irish queen and
her bodyguard on the next full grain-ship
to Ostia, the last in the season.

It seemed that so far down had he slipped in
the esteem of his subjects that many
of them, Greek and Nubian alike, preferred a
foreign woman, a barbarian with
snakes tattooed on her upper arms and on
her backside most probably too. Let the
Romans deal with her and be done with it!
Unknown to the royal alcoholic
the spy of Pompey the Great at his court
copied the letter and sent it to his
master, newly elected consul of
the Republic. Pompey, who had a deep
interest in the East, vested mainly
in the gold paid him by Philopator
shrugged, and failed to see its significance.
He was more concerned with the successes
of Lucullus in Syria and far Armenia,
and, as victor over the Celtic tribes in Spain,
saw little threat to Rome in all this.
The spy of an ambitious candidate
for the Senate, one Gaius Julius

Caesar, however, thought quite otherwise
and slipped out of Pompey's house to Caesar's
with details of the grain-ship's probable
dates of arrival and dock at Ostia,
now only a few weeks in the future.
Caesar was interested: Egypt was
Rome's main corn-supply, but the Celtic lands
were a potential second source: he who held
the supply in his grasp controlled the dole
and was master of the Roman mob, and
now a Ptolemy and a Celtic queen
were talking together. He ordered her
detention upon arrival, but not
openly, to keep his knowledge secret.

The shaven-headed priests gave her a draught
made from seeds of the Indian poppy
and left her to sleep in the deep sanctum
under the wide-eyed gaze of The Lady:
to come creeping back a few hours later
wearing animal masks, whispering soft
nonsense in her ears, but fierce Meadbh woke up
roaring her war cry so that the black halls
trembled with the sound, and the timid
priests fled headlong, forgetting their skilful,

ambiguous lines. Once the sound of feet
slapping on the stones, that of struggling limbs
caught in the crush about narrow doors, and
the screams of those burnt by dropped oil lamps had
died away, she smiled to herself alone
in the darkness, and fell asleep.
The Great Mother Cat of the House studied
her with slitted, green eyes, thoughtfully
left a few dead mice at the foot of the
hypnagogic couch as a snack when she
woke up, and then she sauntered off, shadow
among many others, not all living.

Meadbh seemed to wake but not to wake, as she
was conscious, rigid, unable to move,
a great weight upon her chest as though dead
lions pursued a nightmarish revenge.
She felt fear and panic, as above her
leaned a strange woman whose beauty lighted
the Stygian darkness of the Sanctum
of Oracles: 'You seek signs from Isis,
but the Mother of the Saviour," she said," is
about to enter the womb of the King's
Great Wife, to be incarnated as our
own Cleopatra, and you must leave Egypt

because you are a magnet of power
which may lead us all into a troubled hour.
Before you go, as a special favour, you may
speak with the Fates. Go in peace, but go away!"

At once, Meadbh found herself standing in a
vast room cluttered with metal boxes full
of flashing lights and a low humming like
sleepy bees. Three young girls turned to fix her
with incurious, over-innocent
eyes. Behind them was a luminescent
globe seemingly of crystal or magic
water: at their feet carrying-cases
were stacked. One girl, the youngest, seemingly
about seventeen mortal years in age had
blonde braided hair and bright blue eyes; she wore
red leather boots to which were attached wheels,
which enabled her to speed at will all
about the round room, and even the walls
when excited; plus tight blue trousers and
blouse of many-coloured silk which left her
belly-button visible. In her nose
glittered a small diamond stud. "Peas-Blossom
is the name," she introduced herself," though
you can call me "P". And, this is Cobweb,"

and a beautiful black-haired girl, perhaps
a year older, with oriental eyes
and features, dressed in a tight cheongsam
covered with embroidered fighting dragons
nodded distantly. "We call her Webby."

The last of the trio was the eldest,
at least nineteen, tall and ebony like
one of the Nubians, dressed up all in
black leather with silver jewellery. She
smelled of some spicy perfume. (Meadbh was
avid to get some of it to take back home.)
She fixed Meadbh with a challenging stare:
"I am Moth or Ma'at to the Nubians,
Atropos to the Greeks."

"Where am I?" she asked. P replied:
"This is the Cave of the Fates and we are not
here to help you come to terms with your lot,
whatever it is." She looked at Meadbh with
an expectant air, then with impatience,
finally began to speed up and down
the racks of green glowing machines, whistling.
Meadbh found this extremely irritating.

"Don't you do any harmful spells?" asked Meadbh.
"Spells which lame and blast? Spells which
curdle the brains or give you the shits."

"We just work out predictions," said Moth,
"like the oracle of Delphi but adumbrated
without all their embellishing and hedging about,
so don't expect us to give you a list of winners,
and leave out the Uncertainty Principle,
when we've just got it all nicely worked out."

"And another thing," said Meadbh,
"you're supposed to be three hideous hags,
with one eye and one tooth between you.
Yet here you are, all tarted up like trainee
streetwalkers, with your firm bellies,
jiggling boobies, pert, provocative bottoms,
and too much face-powder and lip-stick."

P put her straight, speeding in like a meteor from the blue:
"Just a poetic tradition. We can be ourselves
in any suitable form, and we like these!
In fact, we are taking them to the Dodecanese
on an extended vacation, and hope time slowly passes
while we have our bare behinds chased between the

dunes by beautiful young men for a bit of a lark."
Meadbh was now both outraged and still in the dark:
"Who'll guide mankind while you flash your arses?"

P laughed: "We've computerized
everything, using the technology
of the Age of the Water Carrier,
Hapi, as they call the constellation
here. All the machines are eternally
self-upgrading through what we experts call
artificial intelligence." P thought that wonderfully clear
and she and the other two nodded cleverly at
each other with satisfaction. 'But in
any case, there's still that poor sad old dear,
Moira, the ultimate Ruler of Destiny.
And she just loves to interfere."

Webby gestured in the air, and from the glowing bowels of
the strange globe projected the image of
a young man in full armour tied to a
rock, covered in blood; symbols and writing
in the Roman script ran underneath the
whispy, wraithlike image: " Here you are," said
the oriental Fate, " Cuchulain, slain
gloriously in battle in his early

twenties." She raised an eyebrow: " It seems to me, sister, that you have nothing to vex yourself over." She made another another sharp gesture, and the image changed to one of a little old lady with long white hair paddling her toes in a pool of water: Meadbh, stunned, recognised herself. -"Especially as you will outlive your entire generation." She gave a bright grin:" Keep away from the cheese, though!" At this, all three girls started giggling helplessly. Before Meadbh could protest this further levity, red symbols of Greek appearance (of course Meadbh could not read in any language, but she had an eye for the trivial) ran around the little image, and distant bells began to ring insistently. "Oops," said Webby," we may have gone overboard on the Uncertainty Principle."

"Reality, you see",
explained P to their guest, "seems to split here.
If you stay in Egypt, Nubia frees
herself from Ptolemy but war ensues.
Ptolemy is killed in battle and all

his family murdered by insurgents
in the capital. You are hailed Pharoah
and begin a capricious rule from Philae.
The Romans under Pompey intervene
and Egypt becomes a Roman province.
This enables Pompey to crush Caesar
who never invades Gaul: the centre of
Roman power moves to the east, and the
Celtic peoples form their own Commonwealth.
By the way, you escape home, at any rate."

The girls exchanged awed glances: "Wow!.
You must be an actual constant from which
the flow of reality cannot deviate."

"What're you babbling about?" asked Meadbh," Should I
stay here, after all?"

"Oh no," said Moth,
"although you have free will, it does not do to tempt Moira."
P pulled a face—"I only hope that
when we get to Faliraki we don't find them
all speaking Welsh. Of course, this would mean that

Cleopatra could never be Queen of Egypt,
even if she survived the short, sharp
Civil War and the Roman invasion.
-Isis would really be pissed off.'

The three chattering girls, grinned at her,
picked up their luggage and vanished without
a goodbye. Meadbh woke up with a headache.
Rapaire sat on the stone wall which held
in the black waters of the Sacred Pool
of the temple and stared at the fat ducks
with his bare feet dangling on the surface.
Beside him sat still the Great Mother Cat
of the House, studying the carefree birds
with equal intensity. Between them
floated conspiratorial plans of
grabbing, killing, plucking and roasting ducks.
For these were special ducks dedicated
to the service of Great Isis, fit
only for the table of Her High Priest
and his sacerdotal cronies. Also
at that comfortable spot, but leaning
against the wall from the other side was
the remarkable Fionn, the Ollave, clad
in the white robes of a Greek professor,

colour-coded with green and blue designs
around the hems to show his status as
a Druid, as did his long, grey hair, shaved
in the front. Fionn was their herald, a lean
man in his forties, fluent in the Greek
he had learned in Marseilles as a student.
He, too, was in on the duck-theft plan and
had arranged for the birds to be roasted
by a local woman for a fifth share.
Fionn raised his grey eyes to the cloudless skies,
and saw a flight of swallows, flown from the
cold of home to the glorious autumn
of far Egypt: it was a good omen.
There were no fat priests about, or pious
old ladies. "Get ready!" he hissed. With a
spare gesture, he flicked some dry pieces of
bread from his sleeve, intoning a rare charm
to attract the stupid ducks. Five of them
changed course and competed to get there first.
The Great Mother Cat of the House scooped one
up with deadly claws, Rapaire grabbed two,
and Fionn nearly fell into the lake as
he seized the other two. All five stunned ducks
were quickly sent to the Paradise of
the Sekhetu A'aru and Fionn stuffed them

into a leather poacher's sack at his
feet. But as he straightened up again a
huge falcon, bearing a swallow in his
yellow claws halted its dive only a
few feet from them, hovered on an up-draft,
and glared with fixed, golden eyes into the
Druid's level gaze. The three thieves, awe-filled,
watched it climb back into the sky with its
paralysed prey. "Was that Horus, Son of
Isis, come to protect his mother's meat
larder?" asked Rapaire. The Great Mother
Cat of the House had climbed on to his right
shoulder where she dug her claws into his
worn tunic and playfully bit his ear.

"Just a bird," replied Fionn," trust me, I'm a
holy man. I know about these things. Now
let's get out of here before we get nabbed."

No sooner had they crossed the great court and
exited through the pylons, heading for
a rendezvous with their cook, than they were
stopped in their tracks by the Ptolemaic
herald, Parmenion. He was not quite
alone either, but flanked by two royal

officers with others following on
behind. Fionn had earlier hoisted the
sack onto his hip, under his thick robes,
but suddenly it gained in weight. Behind
him Rapaire drew in a hissing breath.

" My," boomed Parmenion," have you got fat
from all the feasting? There is more of you
than when you first arrived!" and he grabbed hold
of the Druid's hand and squeezed it with wry
humour. He whispered confidentially:
" A word of warning, my dear fellow, but
my master has sent word that he has booked
you all passage on the last grain-ship of
the season. So you had better start the
packing. Tomorrow I have audience
with your Queen and will formally advise
her of the travel arrangements." Fionn
thought impassively, "Is that all? no cries
of "stop thief", no dragging away in chains?"
But all he said was: " I shall miss all the
friends I made here."

Parmenion looked
at him sideways:" Why not stay? The king loves

wise men and Alexandria is full
of displaced Celts." The Druid made a sign
of dismissal: " I have sworn to serve the
Queen of Connaught and I cannot soil my
reputation for all the knowledge in
all the books in the king's Great Library."
Parmenion shrugged and moved away, with
a wave and a smile at Rapaire, who
gave a big, friendly grin, and said (but not
in Greek): "Go kiss the organ-grinder's monkey,
ye great fat dollop of palace flunky."

As Parmenion moved off, one of his
officers, a Galatian called Conon,
lingered to speak to them, in his own tongue,
a Celtic dialect close to that heard
a few miles from Tintagel. Conon was
in charge of the local heliograph,
a Celtic invention which required skill
in the code of long and short flashes.
"A boat has left Thebes with armed
soldiers to escort you all back under
guard to Alexandria. There you will
be put on the last grainship of the year
to Ostia, where the Romans will seize

you all for interrogation." Conon
added in a whisper: " It will be here
in only four days. Meadbh must act quickly
and declare herself Isis Reborn. All
will support her, the peasants hate the king,
and half the garrison are Celts. Act now!
Or face torture in a Marmertine cell!"
He nodded and moved away. Rapaire
looked dazed: " I didn't know we were taking
over Egypt!" Fionn told him to run back to
Meadbh with this news, while he spoke with the cook
about the ducks which they would now never
enjoy. But the charioteer was now
gazing drop-jawed across the Nile, where a
monstrous beast had appeared. Fionn explained with
impatience: " That's a camel. I've seen them
in the Far West. Only the Arabs know
how to train them, so they control desert
trade. The locals here despise them...." his voice
trailed off in thought. Rapaire left him there.

Meadbh had forsaken the hypnagogic
couch for her cubicle. She sat on the
hard mattress with her thick head in her hands.
The old priest come to note down her dreams had

been chased away with some nonsense about
the Three Sluts and the advice of Nephthys.
When Rapaire and the Great Mother Cat
of the House, broke in unannounced upon
her dry retching, she listened in silence,
whilst the cat pressed up against her side. It
seemed that her ears were ringing with the sound
of a pebble dropped into the pool of
men's lives. Her only comfort were the soft
ears of the cat, and the earnest words
of the youth: " I think that Fionn will save us!"

The next day, while pale Meadbh smiled and nodded
at the supercilious words of high
Parmenion, her silent warriors
packed their gear. Late that same night, while all slept,
they were led out of a side gate to the
river by Conon, and so crossed over
to the unfortunate bank where the dead
thrive, where some local merchants waited to
set off at dawn for the great oasis
of Kharga. For in his youth Fionn, the far
travelling wise man had seen camels in
Tingis of Mauretania, and knew
that the desert came alive in winter

with huge caravans. He had told his queen
that they would be welcome as unpaid guards
for the three months it would take to ride from
Kharga to the Atlantic where the ships
of the Gallic Veneti traders called.

In this way did they escape the fate planned
for them by Caesar. Meadbh took with them some
kittens of the Great Mother Cat of the
House who had three shares of duck to herself,
and this is how Ireland got her cats of
legend. Of her travels across the great
desert, the Berbers still tell tales of a
great queen from the east who wore a skin from
a lion which she had slain single handed.

When Philopator heard of their flight he
played a little tune on his double-flute
and then forbade all pursuit. " We cannot
afford to waste troops in the desert," he
told his generals. "They' re doomed in any
case. Nobody can cross the Sahara.
Look what happened to the Persians." And that
was the end of it.

-Except that when Fionn
tried to mount the camel assigned to him,
it gabbed his tunic in her yellow teeth,
swung him about, dropped him in a fresh pile
of dung, and spat in his eye. The camel
master was most apologetic, and without guile
said that Moira was usually so cute
and well-behaved. But the Druid who knew the
speech of beasts had distinctly heard her say:
"Steal from the gods, would you!" and he was mute.

Salome's Last John

Herod in a rage
cut off the head of the mage
for blocking his view
when she bugalooed through.

The People's Poet

Clutching his top hat
like a chamber pot
he stands in line for his OBE,
and the Queen may spit in it,
or she may not.
We'll wait and see.
Whatever happens he mayn't put
it on his head as he's not
a proper gentleman.
So he concentrates instead
on his next appearance on TV
and the promise of celebrity.
Maybe she'll kick his arse
while he grovels on his knees,
or maybe the corgis
will bite his ankles:
it depends on how big
the column in The Sun would be.
But to the end of his days
he can bare his legs and boast:
"They bit me here and here,
so touch these scars

and you're touching
the teeth-marks of a dog,
ennobled by HER!"

Perhaps the royal flunkies
will chase him around the gardens,
hallooing and pulling down
his striped trousers:
just horseplay, of course,
but a poet needs to know his place
lest a little unearned fame,
go to his unwashed head.
For the English people
deserve the best
when it comes to twaddle,
and, what's worse,
the good poets are all dead
by royal decree,
bound up by sadistic stitches
in Oxford Books of Painful Verse,
dressed like gents in writhing breeches..
So, when he leaves, panting,
via the servants' gate,
trousers torn and muddy,
behind bare and as bloody

as a lion's lunch,

the policeman will punch

him in the face,

calling him a disgrace:

'Your sort needs a lesson, now!'

But he'll grin and bow

and bless his happy bourgeois fate.

Butterfly Tanka

A butterfly in a park in Beijing
dreamed he was a poet,
but I never dream
of being a butterfly.

Jelly Falooda

Smear the jelly
on my belly
and I'll get cruder
with the falooda.

How Hera Escaped from Tartarus

The language of the Titans consists of but six hundred words,

all monosyllables with simple meanings like "go", "sleep" or "man",

and eight tones to express emphatic expressions,

questions, imperatives, tenses and so on. But the Titan

larynx is constricted so that the words are spat out

like grunts, shrieks, and odd squeals which add colour to go

into any conversation, and a subtle nuance to meaning.

Apart from all this, there are sixty gestures and ten face-pullings

to suggest emotions like awe, horror and seduction together with

simpering, slobbering, eye-lash fluttering, ear-waggling and a pitiful keening,

plus thirty-six postures (crouching, towering, shuddering etc),

oral modifiers like stuttering, whistling, singing both high and low,

and six bodily noises: spitting, farting, snoring, hawking, deep sighs

and clapping the hands. Finally, there are the bodily functions

of pissing, shitting, puking and wanking which are never wise

to employ except as deadly insults. (The female version

of wanking involves doing something unseemly

with the tooth of a giant sloth, and shitting on an enemy's

doorstep is an invitation to fight a duel.) But do not be deceived.
The Titans are not a primitive tribe but up to scratch
in methods of communication, including a secret telepathy.
Their culture has an ancient and majestic oral poetry
and, as for drama, a Titanic matinee is something to see:
part ballet, part opera and part wrestling match,
and Hera invented the modern Titanic play
while cast into Tartarus by Herakles, and left to stay.

Hera was sitting alone in the guest house over a bowl of blue
black bean broth when the god Set sat down opposite.
"Typhon!" she exclaimed, "What are you doing here?"
"The wedding," he replied. "Remember that they count me
as a Titan from the frozen north here, so call me Loki now."
(Hera remembered a verbal invitation to some mighty do.)
"Help me to escape," begged the goddess," there's a dear."
Set said she was a prisoner of their laws of hospitality,
and had to put up with it until they asked her to go.
"As they get few visitors," he went on,"you would have to
really upset them some way."
"But how?"

"Well, you could make a mockery of this wedding,
but that might also be humiliating for you, too."
Set flipped back his long black hair with a grin:

"Got to go. I slipped out of the bachelor party to say hello,
but it's my turn in the barrel, and to miss that would be a sin."

When Hyperion popped in to see if she were having a nice
stay,
    Hera announced that she wanted to put on a little play
    as her present for the happy pair. Hyperion frowned,
    being a more recent strain of Titan, he looked like
    a pensive Greek god. "What a nice idea!" he finally said,
    "It would be so improving for our country dwellers.
    But you have little time to train actors, as we have none."
    He thought a bit: " But we cannot ignore the call of progress
    and we do have praise singers and story tellers
    who can remember thousands of lines…Yes! It will be fun!"

All Hera had to do was enlist the aid of the Women's Institute
    and the Gentlemen's Club, invent a theme of the War of
the Sexes
    and suggest the creation of a new sort of orchestra
    and they were well away, with her excitingly avant-garde play.
    For music the Titans usually banged two sticks together
and clapped
    their hands, but Hera added gourds full of stones to be shaken,
    Cretan bull-roarers, bow-string harps, Centaur didgeridoos
    and drums made of dried skin stretched over hollowed-out
logs.

Within a very short time all the spoken parts had been taken,
and excited musicians had developed a strange, brutal rhythm
which sounded eery in their natural theatre, a huge, painted
cave in the hills above Hypostasis, their capital, to which
all repaired
after the wedding ceremony and before the evening feast
and orgy.

The play was calculated (so she planned) to shock all in
that Titanic city,
as it depicted a sluttish bride and a half-wit groom, two
opposing families of vulgar origin trying to outdo
each other with ludicrous affectations and gifts of passe junk,
and even a drunken priest of the Earth Mother at the
ceremony,
who said:" Do you take this bitch to be your lawfully
wedded bride,
you short-sighted, bandy-legged lover of little boys?"And
then aside:
"I've just shagged her, and believe me, I could only manage
it drunk."

Hera was delighted to see that the Titans watched with
gaping mouths
and wide-open eyes, gripping each other as though in disbelief.
When the performance ended with the naked dancers
sticking the teeth of the giant sloth into mutual orifices-

and not even their own, there fell a sudden silence which seemed to rob

the cavern of its borrowed warmth. Hera feared an attack from the mob,

but when the Titans leaped to their feet, it was merely to hoot aloud

and pound their chests. Hera did not realise that she was being applauded,

not booed off the stage, until a little girl in the red pixie hood

all female Titan toddlers wore, presented her with a basket of fruit—

the Titans did not eat flowers—and made her see an awful truth:

they <u>loved</u> it! And now they would never let her go....

She raised her arms in fraught appeal to Heaven and screamed:

"Zeus, save me! Let bygones be bygones! Am I not accorded

help in my time of need by the bonds of our sacred marriage bed?"

And when the deadly lightning was not set loose,

she began to sob and weep, cursing all the while, like one demented.

She failed to notice in her grief that the audience seemed struck dumb.

To pray to their enemies, the sky gods, was a capital offence,

and the one bodily function which Titans could not reproduce

was weeping, as they had no tear ducts, for they dwelt

in a cold climate where tears would freeze. and had evolved accordingly. So tears to them are like hawking and gobbing to us.

From the wings hastened a shocked Hyperion, to appear scowling at the twin insults of blasphemy and public nuisance, forced to declare her persona non grata and revoke her status, which is how she was thrown out of Tartarus on her rear, though her reputation as an innovative playwright

suffered no damage from that shocking finale to a creative night.

Gremlins

One Halloween you may get a knock on the door,
and find nobody there, until a small hand tugs
at your jeans, and looking down you see a grinning
green face and at first assume that a five-year old
is combining knock up ginger with trick or treat.
Then you see the wrench in his hand, and the bold
crowd of other gremlins around the pile of metal parts
which used to be a car parked in the street,
all grinning and waiting on your despairing groan.
And then:" Look what we've done to your car, mister!"
When it happened to me, I said:" But I don't own
a car. That used to be a sporty pre-war Sunbeam
belonging to Captain Apollo of the County Cricket Team."

"O crap!" the gremlin gasped with bulging eyes
and he and his pack fled from the avenging Lord of the Skies.

Gremlins are very inquisitive, and love to play a trick.
They make good friends if you can take a joke,
but bad enemies, if they think you're weak.
I once knew a man in Walthamstow who threw half a brick
at a gremlin on the fourth of November for giving him cheek,
and he woke up the next morning in his bed

with the entire house demolished around him,
the bricks and tiles neatly stacked out at the back,
all his furniture in a pyramid in the front garden,
with a Guy Fawkes made from his clothes on the peak,
a placard around its neck which clearly said:
NEXT TIME IT'S A REAL COUNTDOWN FROM TEN,
and when his alarm went off, the fireworks started.
(He was certified insane by two Serbian psychiatrists,
because he believed in little green men for a fact,
and then shoved in the slammer for a terrorist act.)

They may be small, but they're stronger than us,
and where you see one, there are thirty near by,
so show some respect when they play you a trick
or they'll teach you a lesson like the man with the brick.

In an Alternate Estate of Consciousness

The sleepwalkers of Leytonstone
come back at night to walk their old haunts,
blown into a broken concrete scree
by an explosive council decree.
Their certainty taunts
worn sleepers on damaged beds
bought cheaply from the secondhand
benefactor of bug and flea,
who cannot clearly find their way
by dismal foggy day.

When it gets cold the old will die
and neglected babies will shiver and cry,
and all the safe bourgeoisie
will bless the demographic spell
which fixed for Wanstead
a Tory MP until ice covers Hell.

Trinidad

The Mouths of the Dragon gape raggedly
under the clouds' vanilla canopy
and the Columbus waters catch the eye
of the sun peering over sky and sea
warmly lapping each other. And only
this battered tub has motion beneath my
feet, white wake cutting through green acid dye.
The five storms we weathered rhythmically
have added their electricity to
the brain so that strange visions come flying -
fruit bats with the faces of wild women,
forest shapes moving on shore to pursue
our souls with melancholy, their crying
dulled as the mind begins to awaken.

Grenada

Isle of spice, sweet-scented home of the palm,
washed by the warm currents of the Carib
Sea, home to talking spiders, the ad lib
remembrances of Africa, and calm
days in hidden bays. We walk arm in arm
while rain closes shutters on the restive
forest in patterns of cloud, the trees give
a noise of groaning about the secret charm
of black, haunted Grand Etang, fathomless
shaft of the long dead volcanic abyss,
its reeds silently nodding their knowledge
of ancient sacrifice. Thus, ridge on ridge
the lava mountains march with foreign names
like dragons, their true births written in flames.

Lilith has a Dream and Isis Wakes Up

Lilith, the green-eyed demon,
felt a little funny on the tube,
between Mile End and Stratford,
and had an amazing vision
of herself, a stone giant,
carved from red sandstone,
standing on a black granite cube
in the middle of a town of domes,
arcades and tall towers in open spaces,
built of teflon on Mars, of all places!
On that plinth was carved
in classical Augustan letters
FREEDOM, which was at her feet
repeated in all the literate languages
of humankind.
She'd just laid to rest that day,
her dad, Lou Siefer, as the stone announced, next to his big brother,
Uncle Joe, in Romford Cemetery, under a headstone marked
Joe Hoover because the Romanian stonemason misread her scrawl,
and his Serb boss knew no English at all,

though he'd developed an expertise with graves, quite
uncanny.

Uncle Joe lay there as an Englishman of the better sort,

an imperial gentleman of singular design,

with contempt for his lessers, and filled with love divine

for church investments in off-shore trusts,

a spanker and flogger, adored by headmasters with bestial
lusts,

prison governors and bent chief constables everywhere).

Thus, the family business was, as it were, per se,

dissolved until some aeons thence

when the pair might return from outer darkness

to keep us again in tedious suspense,

for such artful rulers love to press

us down in subjection to their lies,

and feast upon the souls of the lazy and foolish

who buy false promises as charters of Paradise.

Lilith thought, "I'm free at last from the mould,

and can be my own woman if I wish.

I'd like to really be the image of such Liberty,

so now the path of wisdom and courage will be mine."

And when she got out at Leyton,

all the weeds along her path were changed

into blushing roses and sweet columbine,

and the birds burst into joyous song
and passing strangers smiled at sights
and smells of ordinary things
as though tickled by childish delights.
And Lilith got a place in Imperial College
to study quantum physics and dimensional relativity.

At that very moment, in Harlesden,
the Universal Mother, Great Isis,
stepped out of the statue of the Madonna
where Asian women pray to Lakshmi,
and muttered in a puzzled voice:
"This is not the Stella Maris Seaman's Mission
in Markhouse Road, Walthamstow, where I dossed down.
It looks like an entirely different part of the town."
And orienting herself to the rising sun
she stepped off her plinth and began to walk,
while red flowers sprang up behind her through
the cracks in the pavement, and pigeons made
victory rolls around her head. She collected
a gaggle of Hari Krishna dancers, buskers,
choirs from various places of worship
and street musicians, besides many casual onlookers
who became possessed by the Spirit of Resurrection,
Osiris, her husband, summoning her home,

and gradually the wondrous Hymn to the Sun
united all sects and believers into a jostling mile,
fulfilling the destiny of Akhenaten and that other
heretic, Francis of Assisi, and charging the polluted
air of London with the magnetism of the Nile.

"Something new has come to pass," mused great Isis:
"the spell of the Fishy Age has been broken....
and some new player has wiped the smug smile
from the ugly mug of brother Set.
Now shall we women shake out our skirts
and dance the two-step with flashing feet,
and hunt out the prowlers from the titty bar,
and bury them wrapped in the wagging beards
of wise old wankers, judges, generals and rabid priests,
for the New Age has bouncing girls enough
to fill the streets for a magical Mardi Gras!"S
And so the world laughed and sang like crazy,
And danced the Titan hands, knees and bumps-a-daisy.

Poor Haiku

I love litter bins
and the smell of damp paper
when I read the news.

This meat is not off,
just discounted. The freezer
is fine. Well, almost.

This suit does not fit -
somebody dropped dead in it.
Now I have presence.

Reading rooms are warm
in winter, but full of tramps,
who resent my suit.

The Waters of Lethe

The children have all run off into the woods,
hiding from their parents. Daddy has a big knife
and wants to make them fit into a future
like his past: Mummy wants to send them away
to learn proper English somewhere nice
because they're starting to sound
like the children on the estate.
With a bit of luck, the children think,
their parents will soon get bored trying to find them,
and drift back home to pour a drink
of fresh blood. Then they can meet their mates
who live inside the trees and know where the magic
river of forgetfulness runs, and there sip from it,
forget the cramped cudgelling of their suburban fates
and gain a shining knowledge of new realms,
where heroes toil for truth and justice and knock
down demons with a single blow, and have faithful hunting hounds
and ride winged horses gifted by the golden sun god.
For if they forget the lies of adult fools, they can pity
the lost splendour of their true selves, and no longer
need to strive to become estate agents in a ruined city.

Black Jack in the Cemetery

On All Hallow's Eve The Great God Pan
asked me to make up a fourth for bridge
as one of his party of four could not play
on the evening of that special day,
and when I stopped laughing, shrugged
and said:" Then make it Black Jack,
or Scrabble, Cluedo, or Find the Lady,
but I must have a fourth beneath the Harvest Moon."

Intrigued, I let him whisk me away, clinging behind
on his battered machine, and was surprised
to find us roar through the gates into the gloom
of the nearby cemetery, where two dim figures
leaned languidly against a moss-stained tomb.
Both were clad in evening dress (black ties),
and in the soft light I recognised Set, the Father of Lies,
and Baron Samedi, the Lord of the Cemetery, and worse.

Set, a handsome youth with a shock of black hair
which I knew to be dark red in normal light,
shook my hand and grinned: "Now can you boast,
poet dear, of dicing with the universe."

The baron touched his top hat with a grey
kidskin glove by way of greeting,
and so we began to play
with an alternating banker, on the flat
surface of the tomb, and Set was cheating,
or else the rules were like the stakes, queer.
For we used human knucklebones for counters
to enhance the atmosphere, and every stone
angel in that park of the ultimate parting
seemed to turn and stare at us with a sneer.
Then I had to stake my last counter to buy a card:
and as Set slid it across the tomb to me,
all became painfully and horribly clear.

"I know who you are!" I cried in exasperation:
"You are three of the planetary guardians,
called lokapalas in Hindu tradition, and I am guessing
that this is a board meeting, convened to mark
the end of one age and the start of another!"

Set was angry, but hid it well:" So you know?"
He glared at Pan."Well, that's a blessing!"
But the ancient monkey face was unreadable in the dark:
"I told him nothing, selecting a mortal at random."

I went on: "I also guess that the meeting should be really
of two guardians, and two greater ones, called maharajas,
but Hades is on permanent vacation, so Pan is proxy,
and Athena is disqualified by reason of her mundane death,
or rather, the murder of her incarnation,
wonderful Hypatia, by a hate-filled Christian crowd.'
I glanced across at the Baron, who allowed
the monocle to fall from his eye, and pursued:
"And the digestion of Dionysus by the world serpent
has required an ad hoc appointment."

"Bugger me!" sneered Set, "but show that card
that the balance of chaos and order may be renewed."

And at his words the stone angels all around
that silent plot stepped off their plinths to make their way
towards our group with red glowing eyes to surround
and intimidate. "Under the rules," I made my play
(as Pan earlier prescribed) 'I declare the last session
invalid, and urge the re-appointment of Athena."

"There are no rules!" raged Set, an angry joker,
"There are always rules"
I replied, "and I also demand an honest broker."

"Huh! " said Set, "nobody would dare to face my wrath.
Nor is there any god of sufficient rank to judge here."

(By now the heavy treading angels had drawn near
and stood around us in a sinister circle of fear.)

" Then I call upon my old friend, Death. to judge the plea,
for though deemed a minor god in Greece,
together with Sleep and Love, Death is a universal power
and we stand in one of his temples this midnight hour."

"Death will never answer a mortal's plea,"
sneered Set, and now the dread angels reached out for me
but I scrambled on to the tomb and raised my arms
to recite the opening line of the ancient hymn:

"RAMA TERI MAYA JALA BICHAYA!"

For the merest moment the heavens seemed to open
and I looked upon a young warrior in leather breeks
stringing a bow, his hair in a pony-tail,
whilst his charioteer sharpened the iron-tipped arrows
and the god smiled at me and tears ran down my cheeks.
Then came beautiful Death with his crown of white lilies
about his black hair, not surprised to find me there.

One might drown in his wonderful eyes, warm as candle-
flame,

    though his hands are cold like sea-washed granite at Finisterre,

    and I was dumb to his question:"How can you know my
name?"

    finally stuttering:"You are indeed Maya, the Lady

    of Illusion, depicted on the twenty-first tarot as The World,

    and to the followers of the Middle Way, Mara, or Death,

    whose daughters failed to make Siddhartha bend

    from his course, for if you are Death, you are also Life,

    as both are the two sides of the silver rupee,

    with which the Thugs weighted their ritual rumal.

    And you must be the last to find Enlightenment

    because without you, beloved Death, there can be no Life."

Death gave a pretty, musical laugh and was at once

a slim blonde girl wearing a cloak of flowers which she let fall

to reveal a stark nudity:"Yes, Death is a swinger after all!"

At these words all the stone angels joined hands

and, bowing and curtseying, began to dance about

in a gay galliard between the headstones, but the tomb

beneath our feet cracked open and the ghastly figure

of a skeleton in the robes and mitre of a bishop slid out,

and croaked: "Is it time for Resurrection now?"

Maya snapped her fingers and replied:"Not for your sort!"

and the skeleton groaned fearfully and made off into the night
clutching his crozier, and half the angels changed sides
and chased him, one sounding his last trump like a hunting
horn.
He ran until the canal barred his way
and crawled into a drain to hide from the pack
and was never seen again or heard to bray,
though the Waterways Rangers found a battered
skull and a rotten mitre. The story in the Newham Recorder
ran: "Satanists Throw Graveyard Statuary into Canal."

I began:"Come, now, Maya, confess the truth -
did not Set conspire to deny the Age of the Fish
to great Isis, the Star of the Sea, the Pacifier
of the Waters of Noon? And as Athena
was likely to rebel had her foully murdered
in her incarnation by the brutal followers of Cyril?"

"Absolutely," declared Death, reverting to his male form,
"and then he allowed God and the Devil to take
over the world, all because of his eternal spite
against the family of Osiris."Death wagged a finger:
"Naughty, naughty, thrice naughty Set."
Set shrugged:"What difference would it make
to try and deny this ploy of mine? We are here

to change the future, not the past. And there really is
no mechanism to make me suffer for my prank."
And the remaining angels turned and began to advance.
"But I can still prevent you from suborning
the Age of Aquarius, for my last card is an ace to shock
and I now have pontoon, or twenty-one,
and win this hand as triumphantly as any Valmont or Hickock,
for this is even the Ace of Spades", and I turned
and stuck it on the forehead of Death, who is both Mara,
the enemy of all who seek to escape the dread Wheel,
on which turns our Everything, gods, devils, mortals, animals
and stars, galaxies, alternate realities and dimensions,
and lovely, smiling Maya, who puts a brave face on it all.

Mighty Herakles defeated Death when he came to claim
fair Alcestis and gave him a good kicking,
as he likewise treated sad Hades himself who would not let
Cerberus go, but I had to rely on sly magic not prowess.
Set turned pale and the angels sought to snap my ankles,
but I shouted to the pale moon:" I invoke the Uncertainty
Principle
now and forever on behalf of all mortals, so that no more
tricksters
may demand total obedience based on lies!"
The black heavens opened

and I saw the achni devi who guards the great rift

in Time and Space called by the Jinn Rub al-Khali or the Empty Quarter,

from which evil dreams and evil beings seek to invade

our visions, and I put my palms together and made namaste.

And a bolt of lightning flew from her bloody sword

and struck Death on the forehead. 'Oh, very well,' he sighed,

"though there's no need to be unpleasant about it.

You've given me twenty-two million volts. Even Tesla might have fried."

Thus it was that agreement was reached that in the Age of Aquarius

Isis would be triumphant, and Set would refrain from jolly japes,

at least for a time, and not play the jackanapes.

Baron Samedi (who had been controlling the stone angels)

set his creatures to form a conga and jerkily steer

a hokey-cokey through the park. I watched Set fall in behind him,

and heard him say to the god of typhoons:

"I hope that's just an ankh pressing on my rear."

With Death as our witness, we brought in the New Age,

and for dance and rhythm Pan plucked from the air

the Persian Music Channel which was playing Jeannie

by the Black Cats, which we danced with solemnity

until the spell was cast with the ABRACADABRA! in the penultimate stanza,

when we raised our right hands and smacked a high five

just to let the Solar System know the human race was still alive,

and a corner of the space/time event folded back

and we saw God and the Devil at the door of life

struggling to get back in and Kali fighting to keep it closed:

"You can't do this to me!" roared God, red-faced and blue-eyed,

as he was as the headmaster of that public school in Romford,

and in his liver-spotted hand was an alembic of glowing dust,

"for here I have the souls who were all dedicated to me as supreme god,

and you weaklings will never allow them to be swallowed up in the Chaos

where monsters dwell."

"Half of those belong to me," protested the Devil,

but everybody ignored him, the poor mistaken, ignorant sod.

Then the shining sword of Kali flashed and cut off the hand of that thug,

and the alembic fell into our world as the door slammed shut,

and burst like a supernova freeing its contents to be reborn,

even that vile Saint Cyril as a miserable sea-slug.

Across the black gulf, the goddess smiled at us in triumph,

and even sleepy al-Dabaran, greatest of the Jinn, opened a red eye:

"No woman, no cry. None can to Her the Uncertainty Principle deny."

Which was his way of endorsing the passing of power,

not to some Nietzschean Dolph Lundgren, but to Wonder Woman.

For the Uncertainty Principle, you see,

is the formula which sets us all free,

and casts doubt upon such things as fate or destiny,

and kicks the clockwork universe back where it should be,

into the never capacious enough dustbin of history.

I thanked Pan for this chance to win immortal fame,

though asked him to find another to sit in on any future game.

Lazarus Drools OK

After he brought the thrush back to life,
he took some spider webs
and bits of a dead mouse
and breathed over them:ABRACADABRA.
Something nasty with eyes red as a knife
woke up and ran under a rock.
For months afterwards
a hairy, horrid thing killed first the cock,
then the hens in the village,
bit babies in their cots and frightened
women by hiding in dark corners
and hissing, hissing, hissing,
so that they used up a six months' count
of salt to circle their beds.
Until finally the cavalry mount
of the military tribune Gaius Sulpicius
put a hoof on it:
SPLAT!
And all this time he said: "It wasn't me
but my father in heaven" and never ceased
to meddle, and piss off the Pharisees endlessly,
so that the family had to move back to Galilee.
At a wedding in Cana, he turned the water

into one hundred proof poteen and the drunken guests
provided the black eyes and broken noses.
Worst of all he brought poor Lazarus back
from the dead, green-faced and ghastly
and hardly smelling of roses.
Thus animating a three day corpse,
which followed him around in silent reproach,
and sat dribbling in a corner at the last supper,
clutching a bent spoon.
"He must be the son
of some powerful spirit," everyone would sigh,
except for Lazarus who only wanted to die.

Dreaming in Tongues

Sometimes I wake up talking
in an ancient tongue which might be
Thracian or Etruscan and women are shouting at me
to save the city because the king is dead
and the army destroyed
and a babbling Chancellor has the heir
to the throne by the throat
and is talking of giving him to the enemy
in return for our lives.

But I stab the traitor and grab the child.
The royal guards are little older then the boy
and I shout at them to arm even the women and slaves
and man the walls, poison all the wells
in the countryside and promise
our subject states to give them back
all their tribute left in the treasury,
if they'll march. Of course, the sluggards
will wait and watch, so we'll gather
the surviving cavalry for a night attack
when the unsuspecting invaders camp.

And I am happy and eager for battle
because I know that I'll wake up free
knowing that we won, and all came back,
and crowned our prince and kept faith with our city.

Divine Haiku

To become a god
you have to be born in hell
and live for escape.

The rule of devils
will pass, and mortals will find
truth within themselves.

Young, I visited
far shrines, now without the fare,
the gods come to me.

Caverns Measureless to Man

Churning tunes on his hurdy-gurdy, clad in dirty, ragged clothes,

and wailing sad songs through his ruined nose,

corrupt and drunken Silenus wanders beneath my house,

looking for a corner to kip, thrown out by Lilith,

the Devil's daughter, and pursued by angry gremlins,

the mischievous telchins of mining Hephaestus.

And lost down there in the dark, when his flambeau

dies, he feels his cauliflower ear grabbed by an invisible hand,

and falls to his knees, while a hoarse voice hisses: "Gotcha!"

As the tunnels echo an indignant clash of notes

from his music-machine, trembling from head to toe,

he pleads:"Don't bash me, Herakles! I know I'm a disgrace!"

"Don't speak that name to me!" answers a woman's voice,

and the lichen on the walls helpfully lights up Hera's face.

"What're you doing here?" she demands, "and where

did you get those awful clothes, covered in dirt and ripped,

and that rare smell of decay and formaldehyde?'

"I stripped

them off a corpse in the chapel of rest but his whimpering dog put up a fight and chased me to the cemetery gate. I've been damned

because some fool in the car wash jammed

the manager head first down his drain-hole and then walked nude

into the open air. The cops are spreading their usual lies

about me because I've no visible means and should be whipped

until my back looks like a platter of strawberry surprise.

There're helicopters overhead and appeals to surrender for interlude

and my mug is all over London Today. So I'm on the lam,

but you, my queen, look flustered -and have donned male disguise?"

Hera, in the black jeans and flannel plaid shirt she's nicked

from a clothes-line, and cowgirl boots from a shoe-shop

closing-down sale, looks like a 50s Hollywood ham,

a Maureen O'Hara maybe, and grunts:"The mortals've all gone mad,

and, until I've had a rest, I can't worry about how I'm clad."

As she speaks, a small figure in overalls and boots, wearing

a hard hat with a lamp, rounds the corner and gapes:

"Is that you, missuz? Even without your crown I see the boss's mum!"

This is Diggit, the TGWU shop-steward, that is to say,

a local representative for the Titans, Giants and Workers Underground.

Hera has a soft spot for the disreputable little people,

and smiling says: "Well met, good Diggit, now by Moira's grace

we are no longer lost, seeing a friendly face."

But Diggit stares beyond her and points at an apparently bare wall:

"Look!" he shouts:"I spy strangers, and all up to no good!"

The wall fades to reveal a room lighted by alchemical flames,

spirit lamps, you might say, and hands of glory sputtering away.

Four unkempt old men and one ragged old nanny

are bent over curcubits, alembics and bains-Marie,

muttering spells and scrawling with chalk some queer formulae.

"By the beard of Serapis!" cries the gremlin, "It's Mammon,

Azazel and Baal. with Samael and mad old Ashtaroth!"

The erstwhile Royal Guard of Himself look up from their work,

and Samael, opening a fresh export cider can, cackles:

"It's Maureen O'Hara, with that Bulgarian sponger, and a Smurf!"

"Maureen O'Hera, you mean," sneers Mammon,"all trespassing on our turf."

But at the sound of that insulting jibe, Smurf, Diggit has pulled a whistle

from his tunic and blown a triple blast. "I'll have you all in shackles on a rock in the Caucasus, and have vultures bigger than bears

tear your flesh from the bones and rip up the gristle!"

Distantly grows a faint thudding of booted feet, until, with cheers

like a Red Army division retaking Stalingrad, the gremlins flow

into the room, around the amazed goddess and demi-god, and throw

the old devils down, leaving them trussed like turkeys

with rope and duct-tape, on the flag-stones of that now untidy floor.

"Let's chuck them all into Tartarus!" suggests Diggit,

but just then a sign comes from heaven, or Cefalu:

a white dove with a twig of olive in its bill, and about its left claw

a spill of paper which Hera takes and opens up to read

the Linear B script:

The War between Gods and Titans is over! and more:

The world of Tartarus is granted to the Titans in perpetuity,

as part of the reparations for this unjust war,

but any Titan may return to his former home on Earth

and reclaim all property and any compensation which is due—

as agreed between Hyperion, President of the Titanic Republic,

and Zeus, King of the Gods.

As she reads these words to a dumbfounded audience,

it seems to Hera that something tremendous has happened

in the fabric of the universe, and she feels her heart break:

with GUILT. For now she remembers the good things about Titania:

the happy little girls in their red pixie-hoods playing pat-a-cake

in their pre-school groups, the friendly smiles of their parents,

the total lack of crime or poverty, and most shocking to recall:

the fact that the Titans look and act exactly like all who claim birth

from Mother Gaea. Hera realises that a great crime has

been committed in trying to wipe them from the face of the earth.

She falls to her knees overcome by a deep despair and weeps.

"What have we done?" she wails, covering her eyes with trembling fists.

Diggit is upset, and gives Samael a frightful kick:

"Look what you've done now!" The fallen angel protests by being sick.

Hera goes on:"We thought them lesser gods and sought to rub them out!

Only great-hearted Herakles and ancient Pan protected them,

while we were blinded by our own hubris." At this point the dove

flies off, despairing of a reply, and Diggit orders the prisoners removed., but Hera takes note and frowns: "I will allow no torture,

nor crude mangling and disfiguration, nor the damp grip

of rheumatism in some lightless incarceration."

"Missuz," replies the gremlin: " all we need do is strip them bare

and dump them in the High Road for the coppers to find.

They're all born in Babylon, and can be shipped back there.

as instigators of nude terrorism. That seems fair to my simple mind."

"No!" Hera stands up, herself again, and points at the flasks

and beakers quivering with unwholesome flesh: " Don't you see?

They've been trying to clone their old leader by this devilry,

using his nail-clippings and filthy hair. Poisonous Lord

Samael must never be allowed to spread this knowledge abroad!"

Silenus breaks in:" But, despite their aging flesh, the jinn

are hard to kill and may linger on for centuries

until they are released from material form and can return

home to Jinnistan.'

"We call it Peristan, you ignorant Bulgar prick!"

shouts Ashtaroth, most put out.

"Throw 'em down a volcanic shaft,"

suggests Diggit, giving Samael another kick.

But the nearest active volcano is in Sicily, and Hera knows that Athena

would never admit such dangerous cargo to her hold as freight.

And that's why Diggit wakes me up in my bed, for a truly human

solution. "Well," I say:" what would really be a fearful fate

for mortal, Jinn or demi-god, or any itinerant drunken reprobate,

would be to dump those drunks in a suitable detox unit

and get them sobered up and made respectable senior citizens.

Get them to swear by Prince al-Debaran to do the decent thing:

and make an honest living by that Jinn version of the Three Card Trick:

the old three wishes scam. Though, run down as they are, and far from fit,

they'll be limited to performing in old folks' homes

and at kiddies' birthday parties, watching toddlers being sick"

"I love it," said Diggit,"it's so cruel! But you'll have to do the arranging."

And he gets me to find a yellow pages guide, then drags me back

into the caverns to explain. So it is that under the incandescent

marsh-gas globes of the subterranean cavern that the aged loons, swear a dreadful oath, before the great sigil of al-Debaran,

a circle representing a sun, in which are (at the base) a planet in crescent

phase, horns upward, and (at the top) two small moons,

carved in the granite of the back wall above the Great Door to Irem,

the City of Pillars, created from the London clay with a Thousand Gates,

all portals to exotic zones, and rooms to rent at hotel rates.

Then they're bundled up in strips of gunny sacks like pharoanic

clerks fallen on hard times, to be borne aloft by singing gremlins to the nearest

detox unit, which I pick out from the phone-book list and then ring through

to the night nurse: and here my human cunning kicks in,

for I claim to be (when questioned) Euphorus, chief magistrate

of the Spartan Ruling Council, with papers of commital,

signed by the most august of trick-cyclists, with all costs paid at triple rate,

and all details supplied with an authentic, pettish and lordly tone.

But as I hand back to Silenus his mobile phone,

news spreads of the war's ending: Hephaestus, bent over his commission

for a Martian Statue of Liberty, finds himself alone in his forge, his voice echoing from the bare walls:" Come back! You little sods!

Shift 10, you know the rules!" But the gremlins, always suspicious of the gods,

ever the Titans' allies—like Hephaestus himself, who was thrown

from Olympus for secretly arming the enemies of Zeus -

have now raised up their ancient banner, torn down

by spiteful Ares, the Bonnie Blue Flag, with its silver pentagram

inside a circle of lightning bolts. Warren Road opens up for their ranks,

and I, with Hera and Silenus, join Hephaestus standing behind my front wall

to witness a great march past. Mother and son embrace, and Silenus

rushes out to join the gremlin marching band, as the (revised) words

of the Civil War anthem burst out:

"As long as Olympus was faithful to his trust

then just like brethen kind we were and just.

But now that management treach'ry our members' rights does mar,

it's up with the bonnie blue flag that bears the single star!"

Seven times the great column snakes around the block and on the seventh,

the drums fall to a steady roll,and Diggit orders:"Eyes right!"

The music slows to the solemn and ceremonial pace of the kettle-drum.

He gives a snappy USAAF salute (for the gremlins regard the dreadful night

World War Two as their own finest hour) and I see the crippled god weep:

but he replies with a clenched fist salute, and then we three join the column,

though within minutes I get to sit behind an exultant Pan on his Harley.

Events quicken: news of the peace treaty reaches the Titans' world

for Pan has revoked the protective time differential spell,

and a public holiday is declared. Thousands of Titan children appear

behind the massed ranks of the gremlins, bearing their own Red Flag unfurled

with its crossed Sword and Ploughshare within a Wreath of Mistletoe.

It is evening in mid-summer and as we march, people rush with fear

from their homes to gape upon us. Rumours fly thick and fast.

As we enter the lower middle-class fortress of Walthamstow at last, a huge black panther -Mave's panther- pads past our Harley bearing three

red-capped little girls who thumb their noses at Pan and me,

while on our other side, twin boys in the black berets,

with the red star of freedom, which all small Titan males wear,

ride like heroes on the back of their pet titanothere.

From the crowd, an old fool cries "It's the Boys' Brigade!" He asks Diggit:

"Why're you carrying those five?"Diggit snarls:" We're restraining them!"

Which is why the next editorial in the local press praises the Boys' Brigade

for being at the forefront of Retraining for the Socially Excluded.

But others see the flags and red pixie-hoods and another old fool dies

of a heart-attack, bleating: "The lefties are shooting our leaders like flies!"

Somebody uses a mobile phone to tell the world that the embalmed

body of Margaret Thatcher is to be solemnly interred in a pyramid

on Chingford Mount with four of her old cabinet cronies under one coffin lid.

Others insist that Arthur Scargill and the NUM have plundered

the said pyramid and will toss the sacred remains of this modern Hatshepsut

into Tottenham Reservoir as a protest against Thames Water's profiteering.

Thousands of old women in Chingford ram a huge and sinister Queen Mum hat

on to their blue wigs and rush out to do battle with the filthy proletariat.

-But the column turns off to settle on the lawn before the Detox Unit,

and I, Pan, Diggit and about ten gremlins haul the wrapped up devils

to the desk, where the night receptionist quietly pisses herself.

I tell the tale:"I'm the noble Euphorus of Sparta," and here I stick

five bus timetables I snatched on the way in under her trembling nose:

"Here're the court orders to induct them, smarten them up, retrain the bleeders

as clowns, fortune-tellers, stand-up comics, stage-hypnotists and theatre pros,

fill-ins, stand-ins, fry-ups and push-overs and finally to place them in some

sheltered accommodation or half-way crypt to enable their re-entry

into society as hopeless, defeated losers instead of visionary rebel leaders."

I winked:"All expenses will be met from the limitless Iraqi oil revenues,

all five buggers being born in Babylon and failing to be awarded asylum. "

Her eyes keep wandering to the scene outside, for the wicked gremlins have

formed a human pyramid against the glass front of the clinic,

half facing in with nasty grins, half facing away toward the press and TV news,

and many little Titanesses, have climbed up on their shoulders:

here the saucy minxes pull faces and poke out their tongues, by gosh!

sticking small thumbs in their ears and waggling their fingers, very cute.

To the receptionist it must have looked like a scene from Hieronymus Bosch,

made more hideous when, at a signal, the gremlins facing away dropped

their pants and bent over, making the so-called Olympian salute

which they give to any eagle in the sky in case it's Himself, the King of the Gods.

Pan, as if on a school outing, runs over to the window and shoos them away,

and returning, doffs his cap in apology. But this exposes his horns,

and this time she faints clean away, just as the security shift marches in to collect their new intake. Samael has bitten through his wrappings and begins

a plea for instant release, and all might still be lost, but

the outer doors slide open. A scent of patchouli wafts in. Then they're slammed

shut behind green-eyed Lilith, Satan's heiress and Queen of the Damned.

The gremlins begin to applaud, allowing the now half-free devils

to crash to the mosaic floor, and the security guards, spying foreign royalty,

salute with stupid grins, displaying an easily transferred loyalty.

Pan and I, being republicans, bow only to kiss the hand of beauty.

Clad in black leather with silver and jade jewellery and a big beret

with a peacock-feather brooch bearing the mystic sigil of al-Debaran,

Lilith looks like Silvana Mangano in the uniform of a Sardaukar

captain and enough to give any Shaddam IV a palpitationary attack.

"I have a spot on Khalifa," she says in her throaty voice,"and cannot piss about."

She glares at the grovelling quintet:" I'm in charge now, you sorry pack,

and I heard you swear to do no harm in the name of our own Smiling Jack."

Here she pointed at the badge on her black beret, the Red Sun Smiley Face,

as we in the know call the dread logo on the wall of that lost underground place.

They swear again and it ends well, for all obey such a wicked queen,

and Lilith issues her first decree: "When they finally announce

your release, you'll found MEAT, the Mars Exploitation and Areological Trust.

You, Samael, will develop new propulsion systems, Azazel will find the funds,

Baal will chair the plc, Mammon will get the City and politicians on side,

and Ashtaroth will market our shares and pyramid schemes."

"Then you'll run off with the dosh?"suggests Diggit,"and follow your dreams?"

"My dream, you little idiot," replies Lilith "is to found the Martian colony

and then set it free, using alchemical theory blended with Jinn technology".

Turning, she strides out to her stretch limo, with myself, Pan and Diggit in tow,

bending to get in rather low, saying,"Hope you can catch the show!"

and I admiring her leather-clad backside, mutter: "I already have!"

A black thunderbolt with a gemstone collar flashes on to the seat

beside her as the panther resumes the shape of a nude Bastet (another treat)

and an excited blonde, Aphrodite, nips out from the throng to join the posse.

The band strikes up and everybody starts a fresh march to Chingford Mount

where Hephaestus will give a sermon and Hera will be reconciled,

as her plea to Zeus was answered at last by the Titano-Olympian peace,

and had Herakles not cast her into Tartarus, the war would still be dragging on.

There'll be megatheria bearing heroes, and bursting star-shells

a-plenty, thunderflashes and flowing mead, tales of splendid deeds,

calls for the hands, knees and bumps-a-daisy, warlike hounds and strutting steeds.

I and Pan return to my house to watch Lilith sing Qal qalbi, in which she tells

a woeful tale of exile from her desert home to our own uncaring town,

with backing from our own pocket Venus, and Bastet in a borrowed gown, and little Eros claps and cries:"Look! There's my mummy!"

But other darker forces have gathered, too. In no. 10, the PM

opens the closet where he keeps the Head Snitch hanging upside down,

and wails:"The unions have risen, and the lefties are there!

They've hurled Mrs T into the Reservoir and now turn on me!"

Half awake, the vampire suggests:"Send in the tanks to break their ranks,

and gun them down—death to all rebels against the crown!

We lost the class war in '45, and failed in the foiled Wilson coup,

but country house fascism will rise again, and we'll make these nancy oiks rue!"

So at his call, the tanks roll down from Colchester to shell the Mount

but somewhere near Waltham Abbey, they start to fall apart

as the gremlins disassemble them with heroic glee,

stealing the ammo to make festive fireworks to light up the sky

as bright as Baghdad when the cruise missiles fly.

The rocketry spells out, in Titanic (which is the same language you see

on the Phaistos disk) and in Greek: AYA TITANIA, which the crowds read as HEY, IT'S IKEA for some bizarre reason of psycho-semantics,

and it causes endless controversy the next day, many pundits and TV pricks

swearing it was all a promotion for Swedish interior design.

The PM plays his last card:"At least the Bogey Men are still mine,"

and the White Van Men of Essex beyond the Black Stump awake from sleep,

like latter-day Arthurs in England's time of need.

Ten thousand vans roar into the night full of patriots waving baseball bats.

Once again the gremlins strike at the forces of the Essex wastes,

and vans break down all at once from the Wanstead crossroads,

to the manure heaps of Ongar, until a drunken creep

spots some little green men by the lights, and screams:

"The Martians have invaded! Flee back to Becontree!"

So they run away like Circe's pigs, to their garages full of stolen,

and faulty wares and the Bogey Men's trump fails to win this hand.

As the great column winds around Chingford Mount, that true White Mount of the ancient Welsh legends where Bran's sad remains were pickled in brine,

not at that Ludgate named by the Church to confuse our history,

the secret society of sad flagellants who live beneath the Obelisk flee,

abandoning the true Gates of Parth Lludd, they have so long kept shut,

pinned down by the wizard's needle which falsely marks the Meridian ley-line,

believing that Bran the Blessed, Lord of all Lightful Things,

like unicorns and magic owls, dryads and nymphs with a grin, or sexy frown,

mighty heroes who are the sons of Pwyll and Llyr, and dancers free

to know the stately measures of the stars, who are beloved

of the gods, will now pop out from Chingford Hatch and get them down.

And after the show, the Titans go home by this route of Parth Lludd

singing their national anthem: The Song of the Steppes, while their partisans

dance squatted down and kick out their feet, or somersault high

to the accompaniment of Silenus's accordion, and when loudspeakers

from the buzzing police helicopters order the confused spectators to fly, the trees along the street throw out vines and creepers

(thanks to the bulging Bulgar musician) and drag them down from the sky.

And the whole world sings:

"Hurrah! Hurrah! For union rights hurrah!

It's up with the bonnie blue flag that bears the single star!"

And from deep under my house comes the faint echo of the marchers,

their voices passing along the side-tunnel from Irem to the Hatch:

"Down with Tyranny! Down with Unjust Wars! Down with the Ruling Class!",

and "Long live the People! Long Live the Revolution! Long Live the Republic!"

And I can only add my own voice:"Long Live the Republic! Opre Roma!"

O al-Debaran, First Genius of the Stars, may our three wishes each come to pass.

Farewell, Age of the Fish

This has been a nasty time for us all
but especially for the women who got burnt
as witches in droves. There were wars
to declare the greatness and goodness of a devil,
and endless slave raids to save the souls
of children in pagan darkness.
Now, at the end of this cycle,
many loons expect a grinning saviour in the sky
to destroy the world by fire and remake it
in his own corrupt image: but don't despair
for there is no intelligent design here or there
and the Age of Aquarius will play dice
for the universe with chips to spare.

When that evil one rained fire upon
the Cities of the Plain, murdering
women and children
like some F-16 hotshot, he declared war
upon the human race, and only now
is our victory written in the stars.
For no tyrant will reign here
when the human soul makes music,
and mortal feet can dance the long hour

of the Milky Way, and no high-strung
fiddler or pi-eyed piper
can disperse our revelry,
or orchestrate our mood,
or rule our minds
with the smirk of power,
when they point the bone.
All we have to do to shake
off these leeches from our backs
is to jump through the fire at Lammas
and dance the hokey-cokey
around the Great White Stone.
For we are the people,
more numerous than the stars in the sky,
and the only divinities we need
are those of our ancestors, whose heaven
is the camp fire's friendly creed.

THE FIRST TRILOGY
This is now complete

GODS & DEVILS IN LEYTON
A WHIRLWIND IN LEYTONSTONE
LEYTON GREEN

Foreign Words in the Text

Achni devi (Romani): the good goddess, Kali (whose name is not spoken)

Akhet (Egyptian): the Inundation

Almagest (Arabic): a guide, or atlas

Bain-Marie (French): both a cooking and an alchemical utensil for gently heating substances or food, invented by Maria the Egyptian.

Conga (W. African): a dance

Dosh (Romani): money (slang from dost "friend" or possibly dust "shit")

Hubris (Greek): overbearing arrogance which invites divine retribution

Moghkadeh: a pre-Zoroastrian fire-temple found in North Iran and Azerbaijan

Namaste (Hindi): Gesture of hands with palms together in greeting or worship

Parth Lludd (Welsh): The Gate of the Sun, as at Tiahuanaco.

Poteen: (Irish) illicit distilled liquor, moonshine (pronounced pocheen)

Qal qalbi (Arabic): "my heart speaks"

RAMA TERI MAYA JALA BICHAYA (Hindi): literally 'Rama escaped thy Net of Illusion', part of a sacred song in honour of the god Rama

Sambhur (Hindi) a large deer

Sekhetu A'aru (Egyptian): The Blessed Fields, Heaven

Telchins (Greek telhini): mischievous elves employed by Hephaestus, gremlins.

Places Mentioned in the Text

The Black Stump: this is the remains of an oak tree in Wanstead. This ancient tree was cut down during the M11 rebuilding. An act of official vandalism which I trust the Furies will punish!

The Great White Stone: this is a Roman mile-stone just off the A11 roundabout.

The Harrow Green War Memorial: this   is an obelisk erected in honour of the dead.

The Obelisk: this is a much larger obelisk in Chingford, which was erected to mark the Greenwich Meridian.

Would you like to see your manuscript become a book?

If you are interested in becoming a PublishAmerica author, please submit your manuscript for possible publication to us at:

acquisitions@publishamerica.com

You may also mail in your manuscript to:

PublishAmerica
PO Box 151
Frederick, MD 21705

We also offer free graphics for Children's Picture Books!

www.publishamerica.com

Lightning Source UK Ltd.
Milton Keynes UK
UKOW051821170212

187485UK00001B/117/P